BEAUTIFUL

A Sunset Book

CALIFORNIA

By the Editorial Staffs of Sunset Books and Sunset Magazine

Supervising editor: Paul C. Johnson, *Editor of Sunset Books*
Sunset Magazine editors: Norman S. Gordon, *Art Director*
Richard Dawson, *Art Editor* · Martin Litton, *Travel Editor*

Lane Book Company · Menlo Park, California

Beautiful California

In the richness of its diversity, the grandeur of its scenic attractions, and the excitement of its visual contrasts, California stirs those who know it to hyperbole and extravagant appreciation. If Californians tend to write or talk too much or too exuberantly about their state, bear with them—for they are enraptured by the natural beauty of their golden land.

In a very real sense, this fortunate state compresses within its boundaries the scenic features of an entire continent. Seashore, desert, mountain ranges, navigable rivers, waterfalls, landlocked harbors, farming plains, glaciers, perpetual snow, slumbering volcanoes, lakes and inland seas—all are found within the spacious outline of the state.

Most of the state's scenic diversity derives from the unique arrangement of its mountains, valleys, and rivers; its long shoreline that stretches a distance equivalent to that between Boston, Massachusetts, and Charleston, South Carolina; and the extremes in altitude and climate contained within its borders, ranging from elevations of minus 250 feet to 14,495 feet above sea level, from temperature extremes of a chilly minus 56° to a searing 134°, of rainfall ranging from a trace to 100 inches a year, and of snowfall that is unknown throughout most of the state but has been measured at 70 feet on a Sierra summit.

The contrasts start at the surf line. Along its tortuous twelve-hundred miles of alternating beach and bluff, the coast stretches from a sunny, subtropical beachland, washed by temperate ocean currents, to fog-ridden wave-battered headlands in the north—from palm groves to conifer forests. A coastal shelf runs along beside the sea, squeezed between the mountains of the Coast Range and the ocean. In places, the shelf broadens out into open plains or river valleys where the major cities cluster; elsewhere, it narrows to a shallow ledge above the surf, forcing the scattered settlements to cling to the bluffs and the sides of the river inlets.

Magnificent landlocked bays provide natural harbors for the port cities of San Diego and San Francisco; and where the engineering processes of geologic change have failed to serve man's interests, extensive ports have been dredged to form the harbors of Los Angeles and Long Beach.

A series of mountain chains, rising to the 14,000-foot climax of the Sierra Nevada escarpment, intercepts the Pacific's storms and draws down upon the western slopes the rains that nurture the towering redwoods and the thousands of square miles of forest that blanket a third of the state. In the lower elevations, the forests grow in park-like groves of mixed evergreens and deciduous trees: redwoods, madrones, maples, oaks, cedars, firs, and laurels. In the fall they don a bright tartan of orange, amber, and rust, crossed with the dark green of the conifers, when autumn splashes the foliage. In the higher elevations, dense stands of pine, juniper, and fir sweep solidly over the mountainsides.

Within the mountain system lie the gorges, craggy peaks, and the lakes and rivers that delight the eye with their tranquility or overwhelm the viewer with their austere grandeur: the jagged granite wonderland of the Trinity Alps, the gentle landscape of the Kern Plateau, the bold domes of Yosemite rising above the conifers, or azure-blue Lake Tahoe, cupped within a circle of forested mountains. From the heights, the rivers rush down to the sea, tumbling over the cliffs in long, thundering cascades, churning to whitewater as they race through the boulders in the canyon bottoms, and finally smoothing out for the last lap to the ocean.

Nestled between the mountain ranges lie innumerable pastoral valleys, checkerboarded with green squares of row-crops, vineyards, pastures, and orchards irrigated by the natural runoff from the encircling heights or by water piped from the great catchbasin that stretches along the crest of the Sierra Nevada. The vast trough of the Central Valley, largest of the agricultural valleys, covers a flatland 400 miles long and 50 wide in the heart of the state. Rich and fertile, the valley's great patchwork quilt of farms and ranches produces a substantial percentage of the nation's truck crops. A dozen rivers flow into the valley from the encompassing mountains, but only one leaves it through a gap in the Coast Range. The streams empty into two major rivers—the Sacramento and the San Joaquin—and these come together in a maze of sloughs, lakes, channels, and marshlands known as "The Delta" before making the solo run to the sea beyond the Golden Gate.

Behind the mountain barrier, the wastes of the Mojave and Colorado Deserts fill the southeastern quarter of the state. Denied a proportional share of the rains by the intercepting mountains, the barren hills and plains are either seared free of vegetation or lightly clothed with the picturesque plants that are adapted to the hot, dry conditions. Where water has been piped to the parched soil, the desert is shaded by airy groves of date palms, covered with early crops of melons, lettuce, and cotton, or graced with oasis-like communities and resorts.

Throughout this favored state, the wash of spring color offers a memorable sight. Starting early in the year in the desert, the wildflowers and native shrubs and trees give a preview of the coming spectacle with a brief flash of color. The pastel tide moves into the coastal valleys, then slowly climbs the hills and then the mountains, reaching timberline in the early fall, there to bloom until the killing frosts. In good years, carpets of orange poppies or blue lupine cover the open miles of the Central Valley or sweep over the high desert.

Although most of California's visual appeal is in its natural landscape, some of its most spectacular sights are the products of man's handiwork. The challenge of the jumbled landforms themselves has produced the great bridges that span San Francisco Bay, the sweeping highways that snake through the mountain passes, and the white, storied city of San Francisco perched on its forty hills. The viewer is overwhelmed by the astonishing sweep of metropolitan Los Angeles, which turns into a sequined sea at night, and by the interweaving freeways that slice intricate patterns through the limitless city. The visitor long remembers the view of San Diego from Point Loma, the esplanade of Santa Barbara, and the windows of the Berkeley-Oakland hills reflecting the setting sun in a flashing mosaic. He recalls with pleasure the ordered sylvan perfection of the city parks, most notably Golden Gate Park in San Francisco and San Diego's widespread Balboa Park. He recalls the civic buildings that memorialize the tastes and aspirations of the major communities: Santa Barbara's Spanish courthouse, Marin County's remarkable memorial to Frank Lloyd Wright, Los Angeles' skyscraper of granite, and San Francisco's imposing civic center.

The buildings and mementos of California's romantic past add a nostalgic note to the landscape. The growth of the state has been so rapid and all-encompassing that the evidences of the early ways of life have been all but submerged. The few relics that have survived are doubly treasured for the very fact that they have escaped destruction and for the contrast and perspective they provide in a young land.

South of Sonoma, the principal remainders are those left behind by the Spaniards, who occupied California as remote colonists of the Spanish and Mexican empires up to the time of the American take-over just before the Gold Rush. The territory belonged to Spain for nearly three centuries, but the Spaniards left it alone for two hundred years and did not attempt to colonize it until the 1770's. In their eighty years' occupancy, they built missions, presidios, and haciendas in the coastal valleys, close to rivers or to the ocean where the supply galleons touched port. Although these structures were built of soluble adobe and many were subsequently abandoned for decades, some have miraculously survived to the present day or have been restored to their original form. The simple, boldly proportioned mission buildings and ranch houses, with their shaded corridors, verdant patios, and bubbling fountains, still retain some of the gracious atmosphere of the days of the Dons. These fine old buildings have inspired periodic revivals of interest in Spanish architecture, reflected in a large number of Spanish-style public buildings and homes scattered over the state.

The Spanish idyl was too good to last. More powerful nations than aging Spain had their sights trained on this domain, which was known to be well endowed but poorly defended. Russia established a colony at Bodega, 100 miles north of San Francisco in 1812, and the Spaniards were too weak to do more than protest. When Mexico revolted from Spain in 1822, California joined the rebel cause and became a province of the Empire of Mexico. Still remote from the seat of authority, the native *Californios* went their own way, enjoying the hospitable life of the ranchos and indulging in occasional bloodless revolutions. Americans began to trickle into the province by sea and by land, attracted by the tales carried east by the crews of the trading vessels that for years had been exchanging manufactured goods for the hides and tallow from the ranchos.

In due time, the inevitable happened. United States military forces seized the territory in 1846 soon after the start of the War with Mexico. The *Californios* put up a brief but spirited resistance and then capitulated. The territory was ceded to the United States by the treaty ending the Mexican war in 1848, and two years later, Congress admitted California to the Union.

The California that became a state in 1850 was quite different from the California that the armed forces had seized four years earlier—for in this brief interval, the Gold Rush had begun, completely changing its character. The tides of Yankees and gold-seekers from all over the world that flooded into the sleepy little colony catapulted it from the seventeenth to the nineteenth century in a few short years. Population jumped from 15,000 in 1847 to 380,000 in 1860. The center of commercial gravity shifted north from Monterey to San Francisco. The great Central Valley—almost completely ignored by the Spaniards—became overspread with farms and cattle ranches. Towns and cities, roads and rail lines, dams and flumes sprouted suddenly where none had existed before.

The relics of these hectic years are clustered in certain sections of northern California, principally the Sierra foothills, where they decay in gentle dignity. Since most of the early buildings were abandoned after the Gold Rush faded, only a relatively small number remain to enchant the traveler, most of them having succumbed to the destruction of the elements, fire, or the "borrowings" of later settlers. Where buildings were built of stone and iron, they have survived picturesquely to the present day. Unfortunately for antiquarians, the key city of the Gold Rush days, San Francisco, lost the relics of its tempestuous past in a series of conflagrations, climaxed by the holocaust of 1906.

The Gold Rush launched the state on a dizzying course of spiraling growth that has continued with ups and downs ever since. The completion of the transcontinental railroad in 1869 and its extension to southern California a few years later drew thousands of settlers to "the perfect paradise, the land of perpetual spring." Industries followed—oil, motion pictures, manufacturing, airplanes— and people poured in to work or simply to live in this bountiful state.

The floodtide of visitors and residents has been flowing into California for a century, as people have come to see for themselves if the state is as beautiful as advertised. They have come, have liked what they found, and have settled

8

down to man the industries and enjoy the western ways of living. But the tide continues without let-up, and in time the ceaseless flow may someday submerge the beauties of California as it has nearly obliterated the relics of its past. Most Californians have thus far fought vigorously to protect the natural beauties of their state against the onslaught, and it is to be hoped that this restraint will be as vigilantly continued by those newly arrived and yet to come.

Meanwhile, for the long present, this favored state still has more than its share of undisturbed beauty, more than any man can absorb in a summer, or a dozen summers, or a lifetime.

Most of the state's scenic diversity derives from the unique arrangement of its mountains, valleys, and rivers, and its long shoreline that stretches twelve-hundred tortuous miles.

California in Color

This section serves the dual function of presenting the major scenic areas of California in full color and of acting as an extended table of contents for the balance of the book.

The North Coast

A thick mat of golden big-leaf maple leaves carpets the ground at the base of the great redwoods in Rockefeller Grove near Dyerville. The cathedral-like groves are perhaps the most awe-inspiring of the many dramatic sights in the North Coastal area, a forested province with rushing rivers, gentle meadows, and a jagged coastline where ocean and cliff meet in spectacular and perpetual conflict. Narrow, leisurely roads wander through quiet little fishing villages with a New England look or pass the decaying wharves and warehouses of the long-gone lumber shipping business that once sent white-sailed schooners to the far corners of the world with cargoes of Humboldt timber. Often muffled in fog, the coast is just as often bathed in crystal-clear sunshine.

10

Martin Litton

San Francisco

From the air, the vitality of San Francisco seems to take visible form. The compressed metropolis appears to be bursting out of its straitjacket site: the pastel-tinted buildings fill every square inch of land and crowd to the water's edge; all along the shoreline, tentacle-like piers reach out into the blue water of the Bay; and even the massive bridges seem designed to conduct excess energies to other shores.

Fabled San Francisco—holder of the keys to one of the finest natural harbors in the world. Port city, hilly city, a place of chill and fog and of perpetual spring.

Clyde Sunderland

The Bay Area

Harvest comes to the grape country around Napa at the first nip of fall, when the succulent clusters hang heavy on the vines and the leaves are just turning to gold and red. In another part of the Bay Area, Herefords graze on the dry grass of Livermore Valley, still brown from a rainless summer that is about to be ended by an approaching storm.

Such pastoral scenes are common in the green belt that encircles the Bay Area, only a few miles outside the congested metropolitan core. Within this circlet are bucolic vistas of wind-riffled lakes, shady parks and blossoming orchards, and panoramic sweeps from the roads that climb the encircling hills.

Page guide to the Bay Area chapters:

Clyde Childress

14

Clyde Childress

The Central Coast

Framed by dark green cypresses, the translucent breakers of a high tide curl onto the beach at Carmel. Over the hill in Monterey, in the soft glow of early morning, a sportfishing boat churns the multicolored reflections as it stands out to sea.

Not all of the Central Coast is as tamed as the Monterey Peninsula. For much of its tortuous length, the coastal strip is a lonely land, haunted with ghostly fogs and twisted cypresses and echoing to the menacing thunder of the surf against the unyielding cliffs.

16

Santa Barbara

In the richness of its color and ornamentation and the boldness of its scale, the imposing entranceway to the Santa Barbara courthouse provides a dignified setting for the majesty of the law and an ideal background for civic pageantry. The handsome structure is an outstanding example of the prevalent Spanish-style architecture that accounts for much of the city's pictorial charm.

But there are other visual attractions as well. The sheltered harbor, sweeping from a Walden-like lagoon to a busy yacht basin—the twisting roads that climb the ridge behind the city, revealing a seascape at every hairpin turn—and the pastoral ranch country over the hump—all provide vistas of memorable beauty.

The South Coast

Sandy cliffs, smooth beaches, and a gentle surf characterize mile after watery mile of the Southern California coastline. The blue Pacific spends itself on the gradual shingle in a frothy swirl of white lace and laps against the base of the chalky bluffs. When the tide is out, a wide expanse of dark sandy beach will be revealed, strewn with kelp and spotted with barnacle-encrusted rocks standing in little moats of clear salt water.

The warm and gentle surf and smooth beaches draw water-sprites by the hundreds on weekends. Here and there on the brow of the cliffs above, houses cluster on view sites, built as close to the edge as prudence will permit.

Los Angeles

From the Hollywood Hills, the colorful sweep of night-time Los Angeles spreads to the very limit of vision. In the foreground, an audience assembles in Hollywood Bowl, marked by a purple beacon and the eerie light of a vast parking lot. Twin rivers of white and red trace the course of the cars passing to and fro along the freeway leading to Hollywood, just over the dark hills, and to the limitless sea of twinkling lights beyond.

San Diego

The tightly built-up city of San Diego spreads over a plain alongside a great bay so vast in size that it seems almost empty. Scores of grim gray war vessels, tied up at dock or anchored in the open water, seem lost in the great reaches of blue water that stretch for ten landlocked miles to the south, almost to the Mexican border. On the horizon, looms the squared-off bulk of Table Mountain, a few miles inside Mexico.

Port city, navy town, an unparalleled ocean playground, San Diego offers a wide choice of scenic attractions, ranging from the cave-hollowed cliffs of La Jolla to the peaceful backcountry, crowned by Mount Palomar's silver-domed observatory.

24

The Southern Mountains

The mountains in back of Los Angeles offer extremes of contrasting beauty.

On the rocky crest of the San Jacintos, windtorn pines cling tenaciously to the meager soil. Rearguard of the forest, they mark the end of the tree zone and the start of the barren, gullied slopes that drop down to the desert in the hazy distance.

In a friendlier setting, pine-bordered Lake Arrowhead awakens to the rosy glow of dawn, and early-bird fishermen cast off for a day on the glassy water.

Horst Ahlberg

The Desert

The arid, deadly landscape of Death Valley presents a hypnotic picture of menacing grandeur. The barren mountains, colored with the rich browns and yellows of kiln-fired clay, are burned clean of vegetation by the searing sun and deeply etched by the wind and the occasional cloudbursts that sluice down their exposed flanks.

Not all of the desert is as forbidding as Death Valley. Spring comes to the Mojave hills in a blaze of orange, as the poppies unfurl their colors as far as the eye can see. In other areas, piped water has converted the sterile landscape to a green checkerboard of crops, date farms, golf courses, and home gardens.

Josef Muench

William Aplin

The Sierra Nevada

The majestic granite domes of Yosemite rise above
the conifers nearly a mile straight into the clouds,
and the icy Merced River, swollen with the snow-
melt from the High Country, flows swiftly down
the canyon. This is a scene that is known around
the world, has been reproduced on myriads of
postcards and pasted into countless tourists' al-
bums, yet it remains perpetually fresh to the
viewer, whether he experiences it for the first or
the hundredth time.

Dozens of equally spectacular views abound in
Yosemite and elsewhere throughout the Sierra
Nevada. Easily accessible to the perceptive traveler
are emerald lakes, sparkling rivers, forests of
giant redwoods, and, in season, a snowy world of
tingling beauty.

Vincent Thomas

The High Country

A pair of red-shirted hikers pauses on the High Sierra Trail in Sequoia National Park to savor the immensity of the granite world spread out before them, far beyond the road's end. The jumbled cliffs and spires rise above timberline and the last trees cluster together in the glaciated valley below. Ahead lies Hamilton Lake and beyond that (right) the Kaweah Gap, high gateway to the Big Arroyo. On the horizon, 12,000-foot Mount Stewart juts into the sky.

A special province of the Sierra Nevada, the High Country occupies a narrow strip of alpine wilderness that runs along the spine of the great Sierra chain. Most of it well above the 10,000-foot level, it is a barren land with limitless vistas of soaring ridges, deep chasms, and azure tarns imprisoned in granite bowls.

The Gold Country

The hills surrounding Nevada City burst into vibrant color when autumn splashes the trees with amber, gold, and scarlet. Built more than a century ago, the gracious old town has changed little since it was a bustling Gold Rush settlement, and its well-preserved buildings retain a nostalgic air of the 1850's.

Not all of the Gold Country remains so well preserved. The foothills are littered with dying buildings and mining equipment, picturesque in decay and haunted with the ghosts of the thousands of fortuneseekers who spent ten rambunctious years in the diggings and then dispersed to the four winds.

The Central Valley

A solid carpet of yellow spreads under the freshening oaks as the buttercups herald the arrival of spring in the Sacramento Valley. In a southern part of the Central Valley, a lowering sky reflects darkly in the shallow water of a series of rice ponds, separated by meandering, reedy dikes.

The table-top terrain of the great Valley does not lend itself to vistas of spectacular contrast; rather, it reveals its beauty in quiet scenes—whitewashed farm buildings beside a eucalyptus windbreak, a sylvan park fronting on a river bend, or the tule-bordered mazes of the Delta, where the Sacramento and San Joaquin Rivers come together.

John Robinson

The Northern Mountains

Under an indigo sky, icy mists roll off the white flanks of Mount Shasta, completely engulfed in glistening snow. The rough and jagged contours of the peak are rounded over and concealed by the muffling blanket of white. In the foreground, the snow lingers on the needles of a conifer forest turned brown by the rays of the late sun.

Snowy Mount Shasta is a typical representative for a mountainous province that is noted for solitary peaks and steep, alpine ridges. The Klamath Mountains, Trinity Alps, and the southern tip of the volcanic Cascade Range offer a wide choice of scenery—dams, lakes, rivers, and an inactive volcano that still emits disquieting wisps of smoke and steam.

Richard H. Baker

The North Coast

The North Coast is a land of loneliness—of rolling fog and dripping trees, of breakers smashing against rocky bluffs, of dark forests, abandoned lumber towns and logged-off hillsides. But it is also a land of champagne air and sparkling sunshine, a tonic rendezvous for vacationers, a place where rivers run smooth and swift, and venerable little towns with a New England look serve fine chowders, cheese, and wine to the traveler. It is an area that history has touched, as its polyglot place names reveal—Noyo, Point Reyes, Fort Ross, Albion, Valley Ford tell the visitor that Indians, Spaniards, Russians, Englishmen, and Yankees all have had a hand in shaping the destiny of this haunting land.

For its full length, the North Coast is a rugged province where the mountains march straight into the sea and the stubborn cliffs explode the smashing breakers in a spectacle of titanic conflict. Here and there, the coastline opens to an occasional stretch of sandy beach or curves inland to form sheltered coves, beyond the range of the pounding sea. Picturesque fishing villages cling to the sides of the inlets, embracing waterborne forests of masts and spars that rise and fall with the tide when the fleet is in.

Here is the home of the giant redwood, ancient stately trees that soar skyward in softly-lit, cathedral-like groves a few miles inland from the sea. Nearly as old as Western Civilization, the great trees humble the reverent viewer with their antiquity and their majestic proportions.

The works of man add a nostalgic note to the landscape. Most of the ranch houses, barns, and stores were built by an earlier generation with simple materials and from simple plans. Miles of zigzag, split-rail fencing and windbreaks of dark, tangled cypress accompany the leisurely roads. Even man's discards have a melancholy attraction. Abandoned lumber towns, wharves, and mills recall the days when great quantities of lumber were processed and shipped from the once-busy towns along this shore.

Over all this country rolls the intermittent fog, sometimes high and gray and turning everything to monochrome, sometimes scudding over at rooftop, and sometimes clinging close to the ground, where it muffles the roar of the breakers and the rush of the wind through the great trees.

40

Martin Litton

G. N. Pendleton

41

Martin Litton

THE NORTH COAST

The tide smashes ceaselessly against the cliffs, slowly wearing down the stubborn rock an inch a decade. Frequently, the salty spray of the breakers mingles with the fog that forms over the ocean and rolls inland like an aerial tide. The chill mist first fills in the valleys, then veils the dark forests, and finally engulfs the mountain crests in an unbroken sea of cotton. Beneath the fog, the forests luxuriate in the dampness—indeed, the great redwoods depend upon it as a condition of life itself.

42

THE NORTH COAST

*Older than Christianity and larger than any other living thing, the
stately redwoods soar above their forest companions and mat together a
hundred feet above the ground to form a high, vaulted roof. Often shrouded
in fog, the groves are always softly lit, even when the sky above is clear.
Sunlight is filtered by the thick canopy to a dim cathedral luminescence, but
here and there it finds an opening and slants down in shafts of dancing light.*

Richard Dawson

Ray Atkeson

THE NORTH COAST
*Wide, smooth rivers wind their way
through the redwood forests to the ocean.
Some of them carry logs from distant
cuttings to the shoreside mills, whose
perpetual fires of smouldering sawdust cast a
fragrant pall over the water.*

*Enough logs have traveled these waters to
make many men wealthy—rich enough to
build mansions, such as the Carson House
in Eureka, a handsome example of
Victorian exuberance.*

THE NORTH COAST

Visitors from New England feel immediately at home in Mendocino, and well they might, for the town was laid out and built by Yankees in the 1860's; and, escaping erasure by fire or improvement, it remains largely the way it looked in its prime, before the lumber industry moved away. Even the quaint figures of Father Time and the Maiden, which cap the Masonic Hall, wear their years lightly.

Richard Dawson

49

THE NORTH COAST

Here and there a fishing village clings to the shores of a river mouth. The two halves of the village, connected by a spidery bridge, embrace a tightly packed fleet of small vessels moored on the tranquil water. The boats weigh anchor in the misty dawn and chug out to the open sea, returning at nightfall accompanied by clouds of raucous gulls. Once lumber ports, these villages long ago switched to fishing after lumber shipping declined; but the old lumber mills and docks remain, neglected and disintegrating.

THE NORTH COAST (FOLLOWING PAGE)   Rondal Partridge

When the mists roll over this bleak headland, the old stockades seem to echo to the ghostly footsteps of the Russian colonists who labored here for twenty-nine years (1812–1841) in the service of the Czar. A world away from Moscow, they improvised a courtly way of life, farmed, hunted, and traded with the wary Spaniards to the south.

The North Coast

The white cliffs of Point Reyes attracted Sir Francis Drake to a safe landing in 1579, but they have brought destruction and death to less fortunate mariners in the years since. Often concealed by fog, the treacherous coastline exacts a tragic toll of lives and vessels. Even today, despite warnings from Point Arena lighthouse and others, an occasional ship blunders into the trap. Only the sea lions enjoy immunity from the destructive breakers, and bask on the sandy beaches.

M. Woodbridge Williams

55

NORTH BAY AREA
Within the shadow of the purple hills that enclose the Napa Valley, the vineyards march in disciplined formation up and down the slopes and across the wide flatlands, carrying their autumn banners to the very edge of the dark forests.

Joe Munroe

59

Robert Thompson

North Bay Area

Great redwood casks, such as those to the right, hold the raw vintages through weeks of slow aging. In proper time, the wine will be drawn off to produce the "bottled poetry" that captivated Robert Louis Stevenson when he sampled it eighty years ago. The alchemy goes on within limestone caverns cut into the hills or in picturesque structures of fitted stone, whose thick walls keep the interior as cool as a cave.

North Bay Area

Above the wine country, to the north and east, lie higher valleys, filled with azure-blue lakes and encircled with hills mantled with manzanita and oaks. The rowboats tethered to the shore of Upper Blue Lake await the rush of weekend fishermen who will park all over the lake's placid surface. The cool waters of Clear Lake, cupped within a mountain valley, have drawn several generations of vacationers who have ringed its banks with cabins.

62

Mike Hayden

63

NORTH BAY AREA

*On the north side of the Golden Gate lies Marin County, a mountainous
province that reflects the quixotic patterns of its rainfall in alternating
sweeps of barren countryside and pockets of thick forest. Most beautiful of
its many groves is Muir Woods, an awesome stand of redwoods growing in the
bottom of a canyon. Crown of its mountain system, Mount Tamalpais
soars above the clouds and presents the legendary silhouette of a reclining
Indian maiden to those with the imagination to discern it.*

65

NORTH BAY AREA

One of the most dramatic sights in all California can be witnessed from the top of Mount Tamalpais—the conquest of San Francisco Bay by the fog. The fog builds up over the ocean and, seeking to overwhelm the warm valleys behind the coastal mountains, it attacks the only opening in the range: the Golden Gate. The rolling clouds quickly over-run the Gate and the city and send a long arm stretching all the way across the bay to Berkeley. The probing thrust is soon followed by billowing masses of fog and, presently, the entire area is swallowed in an ocean of mist.

Gertrude L. Pool

North Bay Area

Boats moored to the front porches of seaside homes—sails passing sedately over the water—houses built into the steeply ascending hills, windows faced to the sweep of the entire Bay—these are the attractions that make the northern shore of the Bay a premium place to live. Off the Tiburon Peninsula, small craft glide over the placid water of a landlocked lagoon, and larger sailing and power boats await the call to explore the open reaches of the Bay and the ocean beyond the Gate.

The East Bay Area

The pageantry of San Francisco Bay can be seen in all its majesty from the crest of the Berkeley-Oakland hills.

When rain clouds break up at sunset, the dome of heaven lights with the fires of the dying sun and the Bay mirrors them in molten splendor. On another day, fingers of fog may be seen stealing across from the Golden Gate, soon to be followed by swift cottony envelopment for the Bay and the hills as well. On a summer afternoon, the water reflects hot blinding sunlight back into the thousands of windows that face it, blinkered, shuttered, and louvered against the shimmering glare.

At night, the lights along the eastshore twinkle in the misty darkness, and San Francisco glows with a pearly luminescence. The darkened Bay mirrors the sparkling lights of the cities along its rim and the topaz-spangled bridges that span it, and when the full moon rises, the water turns to polished silver.

This changeable pageant has attracted residents to the East Bay for nearly a century, and homes are tightly packed onto every view lot all the way up to the crest of the ridge, where they are stopped by the boundary of a regional park.

On the flatland at the foot of the range are beauty spots of less spectacular nature but of undisputed attraction. The campus of the University of California reflects in its sylvan repose the virtues of the classic plan upon which it has been developed. Architectural styles of different eras are happily absorbed in the groves of eucalyptus or isolated from each other by folds in the Berkeley hills.

Another man-made beauty spot, Oakland's Lake Merritt offers a restful retreat in a busy city. A wooded park surrounds the tidal inlet with landscaped promontories, leisurely walks, and jaunty little marinas.

On the other side of the ridge lies a contrasting world, drier, more open and less urbanized. It is a rolling pastoral countryside where shaded suburban settlements are interspersed among walnut groves, field crops, and dairy pastures. Farther to the east rises the sentinel of the East Bay, Mount Diablo, from whose summit more territory can be viewed than from any other point in the Bay Area.

John Robinson

ASUC Graphic Arts

Kaiser Graphic Arts

71

EAST BAY

Late in the afternoon of a stormy day, the brooding Bay spreads a sheet of pewter under a swirling mass of dark clouds. On another day, the water may sparkle in bright sunlight or glow with the reflected fires of sunset or disappear entirely under a blanket of fog

Rondal Partridge

73

Les Flowers Jr.

EAST BAY

A wooded parkland, partly natural, partly man-made, runs along the crest of the East Bay ridge and spills over into the hilly country beyond. Lakes, reservoirs, and golf courses are close by, yet miles away in atmosphere. Ducks float serenely on the waters of quiet little Jewel Lake, rimmed by reeds and eucalyptus groves. All along the ridge are stands of coughdrop-scented eucalyptus, planted like row-crops to protect residents and golfers from wind and, with less success, fog.

Vernon D. Sutcher

EAST BAY

Half of the view from the Berkeley hills is the flatland section of the city itself, which sweeps to the edge of the bay in a mosaic of rooftops and trees. At times, the horizon is hedged in by fog that obscures the sun and drifts off the bay to collect in the lowlands, then rises to cover the hulk of Albany Hill, and eventually to envelop the Berkeley hills themselves. A procession of cloud shadows mottles the flatland and highlights the University of California campus, a city within a city.

76

ASUC Graphic Arts

EAST BAY

*Framed in spring cherry blossoms, the classic Campanile of the University of
California symbolizes the aspirations of the academic community spread
out at its base. It is also the symbol for college life itself that is carried in
the hearts of all Old Blues who passed it on their way to classes or heard
its mellow chimes call out the intervals of their campus stay. Under the
spell of an early morning mist, the normally busy esplanade at the foot of
the tower quietly awaits the sun and the start of a new day.*

Robert Hollingsworth

EAST BAY

*In the heart of downtown Oakland, the junction of five streets in one
intersection creates unusual planes and angles that make the business buildings
appear on the verge of colliding. Only a few blocks from this busy crossing
is 155-acre Lake Merritt, a refreshing retreat where Oaklanders come to
stroll the grassy shores, enjoy the wooded parks, or visit the galleries and
museums along its rim. When not criss-crossed by dozens of tiny sailboats,
the smooth surface of the lake mirrors the hotels and apartments and the
striking Kaiser Building standing along the shore.*

Les Flowers Jr.

81

EAST BAY

Behind the Richmond-Oakland hills lies a peaceful, slow-paced country. The roads meander casually along between pastures and hilly fields of wheat or beside uncleared acres, still covered with the native oaks and chaparral. A dry land, infrequently drenched by rain or fog, it enjoys a few weeks of emerald spring and then turns to dry, rustling gold for the balance of the year. This is a land that time has forgotten. People came here years ago, mined it for coal, failed, and moved on, leaving behind ghost towns and sad little graveyards.

Frances Coleberd

San Francisco

No city in California—and few in the world—can equal the scenic beauty of San Francisco. Built on the hilly tip of a peninsula, its uneven terrain gives it unique three-dimensional form. A city of many moods, induced by the hourly changes of weather, it may glisten in sparkling sunshine, its cubical buildings distinctly delineated in the clear air; or it may lie partly swathed in cloud shadow and partly exposed in bright sunlight; or, fog may steal across, casting a thin veil between one neighborhood and the next or flowing down off the hills to obliterate everything in sight.

The hills open countless vistas of rollercoaster streets, swooping up and down; of the jaunty little cable cars clambering up the rises; of patches of the Bay, the East Bay hills, or the green shores of Marin, viewed at the end of long defiles of close-packed buildings.

A port city, its harbor is visited by a procession of freighters and ocean liners. White, black, and rusty red, flying the colors of every nation, they pass through the Golden Gate and come gingerly to berth at the Embarcadero. Lean fighting ships pass under the bridge, their decks packed with white-hatted sailors, momentarily marveling at the grandeur of the city while they restlessly await their shore passes.

To the north and east, the great bridges hang over the water, suspended from heavy steel cables, monuments to the imagination and daring of the men who dreamed them into reality. The orange towers of the Golden Gate Bridge are often shrouded in the fog that funnels through the slot, sometimes high enough to erase the tops of the towers, sometimes pouring through like a river just under the roadway, and sometimes engulfing everything in blinding mist. The majestic Bay Bridge, less spectacularly sited than its companion, compensates by the grand scale of its soaring leap across the wide Bay.

Once a dozing Spanish village, San Francisco became the emporium of a new world when the Gold Rush exploded in its midst. Overnight, the little settlement grew into a boisterous, frenetic metropolis. The energy that the venturesome Fortyniners and their successors poured into the city gave it a head start over the others on the coast. It grew and prospered, suffered the catastrophic fire and earthquake of 1906, and recovered to continue its growth. Few relics of the early days have survived the fire or the needs of civic growth, but the Gold Rush energy lingers in a shadowy form, nurtured by a stimulating climate and an inspirational setting.

Richard Dawson

Blair Stapp

85

SAN FRANCISCO

From the top of Twin Peaks, the white, magic city of San Francisco lies spread out before the eye, its tall business structures rising like castle towers in the distance.

In the foreground, the hills are tightly packed with a mosaic of diced buildings. Market Street cuts a wide gash through the chiseled landscape to the bay.

George Knight

SAN FRANCISCO

Roiling waves smash fruitlessly against the base of Mile Rock lighthouse, trying to drive it from its sentinel post outside the Golden Gate, where it has stood guard since 1906, protecting vessels from the lethal shoals. The dramatic and graceful bridge arches over the Gate—narrow entrance-way for vessels bearing cargoes from every port, for the swirling fogs that funnel through the breach, and for the winds that excite the water to whitecaps and send the sailboats flying with billowed canvas.

SAN FRANCISCO

As the sun sinks into the fog-shrouded Golden Gate, it projects the profile of a business block onto a path of molten gold streaking across the bay and silhouettes the monumental sweep of the Bay Bridge. The living steel of the bridge vibrates to a torrent of homeward-bound commuters, riding high above the shimmering water.

90

David Muench

Frances Coleberd

San Francisco

From all ports of the world come coffee, tea, and spices; Koala bears, cameras, and stainless steel; furniture and sports cars, moved from the ships' holds to the docks in a never-ending stream. In exchange, the holds are refilled with cotton, wine, and oranges, frozen foods, cement, and wheat, rice and olive oil from the fields and factories of California. At the passenger docks, an immense ocean liner as large as a small city is gingerly warped into a berth by pygmy tugs that strain against the powerful pull of the currents and the inexorable momentum of the big ship itself.

Richard Dawson

SAN FRANCISCO

*Contrasts in the financial district: a tranquil lunch hour on an island at
the confluence of three major streets—and only a block away, the noon
outpouring of pedestrians and automobiles rushes down Montgomery Street.*

95

Hal Roth

SAN FRANCISCO

A little-known face of Chinatown appears in this delightful scene, where scrubbed and immaculate children twirl their partners in a folk dance before a gallery of admiring families and friends. A few steps down the hill, the Chinatown that most visitors know hurries along busy Grant Avenue. At night, the avenue takes on an air of mystery and excitement under the gaudy signs and strings of lanterns. Bright neon invites the visitor to sample the excellent food or buy the exquisite handwork of the Orient. Shop windows display strange and implausible vegetables, meats, and packaged goods. Tantalizing odors of incense, sandalwood, lacquerware, and unfamiliar seasonings roll out the open doors.

George Knight

San Francisco

A white, billowing fog of a summer afternoon, driven inland by a stiff salt breeze, runs over the hills like a band of frantic wraiths. Pockets of the city stand momentarily aloof from the advancing hosts, but they too will soon be swallowed up. At times, the cloud cap settles on the hilltops, enveloping them in a thick, ghostly soup as wet as rain.

SAN FRANCISCO

A cluster of high-rise apartments on top of Nob Hill looks down on the wooded acres of the Army's Presidio, a veritable forest within the city. Just outside the Presidio gate, the crumbling lath and plaster of the noble old Palace of Fine Arts (1915) awaits the hand of the restorer.

101

Glenn Christiansen

SAN FRANCISCO

*Under full sail, racing yachts skim over the whitecaps just inside the
Golden Gate, taking advantage of a brisk 20-knot wind pouring through
the narrow strait. A paradise for skilled yachtsmen, the bay tests their
seamanship with its strong winds and powerful tides. In a quieter vein, the
ocean draws swimmers and surfers to the invigorating embrace of the breakers
along the western edge of the city. Sunworshippers and picnickers dot the
wide beach that runs for three miles alongside the Great Highway.*

Carroll C. Calkins

SAN FRANCISCO
*Down the curve of a quiet path in Golden Gate Park, mother and children
stroll into the misty glow of the setting sun, savoring their peaceful isolation
from a crowded city. In sharp contrast, jaunty cable cars bursting with
passengers clang their way up and down the steep ramp of California Street,
rising from the canyons of commerce below.*

George Knight

SAN FRANCISCO

In closed ranks, the houses march straight up the hillside, obedient to the regimented street system applied to most of the city's forty hills. The homes huddle together on their narrow lots, their windows faced towards the view and the morning sun. In the background, behind a gauzelike curtain of fog, the towers of the business district await their turn in the sun. On Telegraph Hill, the houses cling tenaciously to ledges in the cliffside, hanging on desperately to preserve a view that is well worth the daily ascent of endless flights of steep steps.

Frances Coleberd

SAN FRANCISCO
*Along Fisherman's Wharf, the tough but graceful little fishing craft bob
and weave at the dock, straining to return to the hunt beyond the Golden
Gate. At the Marina yacht harbor, the tethered boats don a festive air
during the Christmas season. Jeweled strings of colored lights, and even a
lighted tree lashed to the truck, are reflected in a dazzling smear of red, blue,
green, and orange on the dark water of the bay.*

The Peninsula and South Bay Area

Down the spine of the San Francisco Peninsula runs one of the most scenic drives in the Bay Area. The road slices through miles of conifer forest, rises and dips with the contours of the hogback, and passes openings in the wall of trees that reveal breathtaking vistas of the ocean on one side and of the Bay on the other.

On the ocean side, a succession of heavily-wooded ridges recedes into the blue distance, melting into the shimmering sea. Few signs of human habitation are visible: an occasional roadhouse, a plume of smoke from a cabin chimney, or a dirt road disappearing into the pines.

To the east, the forest drops abruptly away to a wide shelf, solidly checker-boarded with streets and buildings, that spreads to the edge of the Bay. Beyond is the sparkling silver of the water and beyond that are the dry hills of the opposite shore—the Contra Costa.

The wooded western half is a place to play, and visitors throng its forested parks and swimming beaches. Along the rocky coastline, scores of doughty fisher-men cast into the surf from perilous perches on the spume-flecked rocks.

The eastern half is a place to live, and its shaded streets are lined with pleasant homes and verdant gardens aglow with floral color. Heart of the area is the 5,000-acre campus of Stanford University, a refreshing pastoral island in a sea of residential and commercial envelopment.

At the base of the Peninsula and below the marshy tip of the Bay, a long and fertile valley stretches for many level miles between flanking mountain ranges. In spring, the valley bursts out in waves of pink, as the orchards unfurl their blos-soms, or in miles of rich brown earth, freshly furrowed for the truck crops that are to come. Atop the accompanying mountains, the silvery domes of Lick Ob-servatory can be seen to sparkle when the sun strikes them. Farther south, the jumbled rocks of Pinnacles National Monument attract the curious because of their fantastic domes, spires, caverns, and tunnels.

Russell Angel

Karl Obert

111

Hank Kranzler

THE PENINSULA

Of a summer's afternoon, a thick quilt of fog backs up against the skyline ridge, glistening in the sun under a clear blue sky. Sometimes, the cloud mass simply rests on the ridge, riding high above the towns and forests to the west but shrouding the crest with impenetrable mist. On other days, the mass builds up until the ridge can no longer restrain it, and it spills over in billows of fleece that swiftly engulf the hills and valleys and tranquil Crystal Springs Reservoir.

112

Martin Litton

THE PENINSULA

The buff sandstone buildings of Stanford University have long been one of the Peninsula's major attractions. The sturdy proportions and reassuring scale of the buildings convey more than a hint of mission influence in their tiled roofs, long arcades, and quadrangular layout. Focus of the campus is the 280-foot Hoover Tower; but most famous of the university's many features is the striking Venetian mosaic of the Sermon on the Mount that glows on the façade of the beautiful Memorial Church.

THE PENINSULA

Along the bayshore, the vistas span extremes of barren emptiness and verdant fullness. A sheet of still water spreads for many desolate miles over the southern reaches of the tidal shallows, reflecting with little distortion the lonely towers of a radio station standing beside a salt pond. Two or three miles to the west, the homes and business structures of the teeming Peninsula are fitted into the natural parkland, dominated by lordly oak trees. Particularly appropriate to the area, the landscaped grounds of Sunset Magazine reflect the magazine's interest in blending garden and home design.

THE PENINSULA

Along the ocean side of the Peninsula, the cliffs march out into the sea or retreat behind broad strips of beach, and the waves smash against the exposed promontories or roll harmlessly up the gradual shingle. The treacherous shoals are marked with warning lights, such as the gleaming white tower on Pigeon Point (named for a clipper wrecked there in 1853); but where the beaches open wide, as at Montara, the sand and tide are often crowded by sunners and swimmers, drawn by the tamed, if chilly, surf.

118

THE PENINSULA

The mind finds peace or mystery within the boundaries of the protected forests just outside of Santa Cruz. A silvery veil of water cascades down the rocks in Big Basin park, falling into a primeval pool whose ancient redwoods and ferns and living trunks of fallen trees seem older than Man himself. Along a path in Cowell Memorial two youngsters stroll, alert, walking into who-knows-what adventure and savoring first-hand the mystery and majesty of unspoiled nature.

SOUTH BAY

In spring, the orchards put on their annual spectacle. Like massed Christmas trees lit with incandescent white, pink, and rose, the square miles of apricot, walnut, and prune brighten the flat valleys for a climactic week or two. Farther south, in the long Salinas Valley, endless rows of tomato plants burgeon in the fertile soil. In the open immensity of a valley ranch, a file of weed-pickers patrols the limitless furrows.

William Aplin

124

Richard Dawson

SOUTH BAY AREA

*To walk about San Juan Bautista's quiet plaza is
to walk through the California scene of 150 years
ago. The restored Mission, homes, and hotels seem
to be waiting for the return of the Governor of
Mexican California from the capital at Monterey,
the gathering of the Indians to celebrate the Mass or
to join in a lively fiesta in the grounds behind the
Mission, or, in a later day, the noisy arrival of
the Concord stage from Los Angeles, rolling into
the plaza in a swirl of dust.*

125

Gertrude L. Pool

SOUTH BAY AREA

The tawny hills of summer unfold to the summit of Pacheco Pass, gateway to the Central Valley on the other side of the clouded horizon. The bales of freshly cut hay, dispersed over the dry fields, bake in the scorching sun. Farther south, the incredible jumble of the Pinnacles rears into the sky.

126

Richard Dawson

127

The Central Coast

The Central Coast, stretching from Monterey to Morro Bay, runs a gamut from crowded seaside resorts to empty miles of nothingness, from smooth accessible beaches to tall cliffs that drop straight down into the sea, and from dark-forested mountains to desert-like hills dotted with yuccas.

"The one common note of all this country," observed Robert Louis Stevenson, "is the haunting presence of the ocean. Everywhere, even in quiet weather, the low, distant, thrilling roar of the Pacific hangs over the coast and the adjacent country like smoke above the battle."

The call of the ocean draws people to this beautiful coast to swim in the chilly surf, perhaps to sun in the tangy air, or simply to take in the unspoiled beauty of the white beaches spreading at the base of the dark, menacing forests.

Offshore, flocks of screeching gulls wheel and dive for food carried on the tide or smashed out of rocky sanctuaries by the waves. Sea lions, matted together on the rocks, call out in stentorian bellows that can be heard above the roar of the breakers.

At the northern end of this coastal province, the city of Monterey spreads along the shore of a crescent-shaped harbor, edged with piers, canneries, and restaurants and populated with fishing boats that come and go with an air of self-importance.

Ever since its curving bay was discovered and claimed for the King of Spain by Cabrillo in 1542, Monterey has been a fixture in the history of California. A scattering of restored adobes reminds the visitor of the proud days when it was the capital of Spanish Alta California and the center of a colorful social and political swirl that lasted for 70 eventful years, from 1775 to 1846.

Around the square-shaped Monterey Peninsula, a scenic road winds past neatly groomed estates, golf courses, and resorts to reach Carmel-by-the-Sea, a picturesque town founded in 1915 by a group of artists and writers and still vigorously defending its individualism against the encroachments of commerce. Beyond Carmel, the coast runs past spectacular Big Sur and then takes off on the lonely and dramatic 125 miles to Morro Bay.

128

Richard Dawson

Clyde Childress

129

Richard Dawson

CENTRAL COAST

Fascinated diners watch the ever-changing panorama of Monterey Bay and its flotilla of white fishing boats. Fishermen clean and repair their nets spread out on the docks. A boat sweeps confidently into port, trailing a frothy wake that causes every boat to roll and dance when struck by the widening wave. The piers vibrate to the rhythmic slap of the waves, the smash of an occasional wake, and the bumping of moored hulls against the piling. The heady air is a thin chowder of salt spray and fish odors.

Morley Baer

CENTRAL COAST

The age of the Dons lives on in the Monterey Peninsula. Carmel Mission, with its ancient plantings and mellowed walls, looks much as it did when it was the capital of the mission chain 160-odd years ago. Rebuilt after decades of neglect, it is a fitting resting place for Fr. Junipero Serra, founder of the California missions. In Monterey, the carefully restored homes of the Californios, some a cross between Yankee salt-box and Spanish casa, reflect the gracious and hospitable life that they sheltered.

Richard Dawson

CENTRAL COAST

A restless surf boils on the white sands of Carmel Beach, curving into the distance under the shadow of the brooding, wooded hills. The soft sand records every foot and is pockmarked with the prints of the thousands who have come here to enjoy the sun, the tonic air, and the bracing chill of the surf. A magnificent beach for walking or horseback riding, the hardpacked sand within the tidal reach stretches for miles along the coast.

135

CENTRAL COAST

On a bright and cloudless day, graceful, fleet Mercuries fly before the wind off the coast of Del Monte. On shore, a reverent gallery surrounds a green on Pebble Beach Golf Course, looking, in the long shadows of the late afternoon sun, like Druids celebrating a primitive rite. The crowd stands in agonizing silence, holding its collective breath, awaiting the stroke and the fateful roll of the ball.

Julian P. Graham

137

Josef Muench

CENTRAL COAST

The struggle for survival rages along the coast under conditions of haunting beauty. A twisted old cypress, silhouetted against the dying sun, seems to be resting between rounds in its eternal bout with the wind and the gray surf, moving idly below. Screaming seagulls wheel and dive into the boiling surf off Point Lobos, seeking the marine animals carried by the incoming tide or dislodged from their rocky refuges by the smash of the waves.

Wynn Bullock

CENTRAL COAST

The crisp, disciplined contours of Rainbow Bridge contrast dramatically with the desolate land beyond. Once past the bridge, the lonely highway trails off into the misty distance, crossing bleak headlands locked in eternal conflict with the raging sea. In a lonely valley, a chill fog gathers under the slanting rays of the late afternoon sun and rolls down the hillside like an advancing army of ghosts.

140

David Muench

141

Theodore Osmundson

CENTRAL COAST

This hard land is littered with melancholy monuments to men's attempts to wrest a living from the rocky soil. A forlorn ranch house, framed in the skeletal branches of a wind-torn tree, epitomizes the struggle that more than one family has endured in an attempt to live in isolation, several days' buggy ride from supplies, medicines, even neighbors. But while men come and go, the native plants live on and on: a luxuriant growth of stonecrop draws sustenance from the decaying trunks of long-dead cypresses.

CENTRAL COAST

The Santa Lucia Mountains form a rugged backdrop for the Hearst Castle at San Simeon. The strange but glamorous collection of mansions, terraced gardens, pools, exotic trees, sculpture, and outbuildings crowns a mountain spur facing the Pacific Ocean. The baronial Casa Grande dominates the fabulous estate with its cathedral-like façade and twin bell towers of Spanish Renaissance design. Once the headquarters of the late William Randolph Hearst, the richly furnished castle is now a state park, open to the public.

144

Santa Barbara

In 1786 an altar candle was lit at the dedication of Mission Santa Barbara. To-day, this flame is still burning, having never once been snuffed out. In a sense, this continuous speck of light symbolizes Santa Barbara itself, for alone of all the major California cities, it has been able to keep alive a vital connection with its Spanish heritage.

The Spanish motif is plainly discernible throughout the city. In addition to a dozen lovingly restored adobes and the impressive Mission itself, a number of Spanish-style homes, shops, and civic structures perpetuate the Hispanic architecture in latter-day form. Spanish street names—De la Guerra, Carrillo, Cañon Perdido, Indio Muerto—memorialize pioneer families or events that occurred in early days. And every August, when the full moon sails over the bay, the city turns back the years and revisits its romantic past for several days of spirited and colorful pageantry.

For nearly a century after its founding in 1782, Santa Barbara enjoyed a relaxed and prosperous existence. Land holding families, grown wealthy from the hide-and-tallow trade, maintained townhouses where they carried on a courtly and hospitable way of life. It was a leisurely life, with plenty of time for fiestas and fandangos, bull and bear fights, horse racing, and costumed cavalcades that swept over the countryside to visit the ranchos. In time, the pastoral idyl ended; but many of the *rancheros* stayed on, carrying forward the old traditions as best they could. Some of the city's first families today are directly descended from these proud *Barbareños*.

The beautiful natural setting, which attracted the original Spanish colonists and later settlers as well, is a tree-shaded, hilly plain that lies between the backdrop of the sheer Santa Ynez Mountains and the shore of a gently curving bay. Spread over the irregular terrain, the city's verdant gardens and gracious homes convey an air of spaciousness and quiet comfort. Along the waterfront, a broad palm-lined esplanade runs from a still lagoon, where waterfowl live in open sanctuary, to a busy yacht basin, where white boats bob up and down with the rhythm of the tide.

Over the crest of the Santa Ynez range, a world of rolling ranchland spreads over the oak-shaded hills where vaqueros once raced after gawky, long-horned cattle or lassoed grizzlies for harassment at the next fiesta.

Martin Litton

V. Earl Lewis

147

Martin Litton

Santa Barbara

Under a full moon, a ghost fleet rides at anchor on the dark waters of the harbor. The mixture of pleasure craft and fishing vessels bobs restlessly to the slap of the wavelets. Soon, dawn will release half of the restive flotilla, and the fishing boats will chuff out to sea. At sunrise, the service pier stands high above the low tide on ungainly piling, reflected darkly in the moving water. Activity is suspended, awaiting the rise of the tide, the turn of another day.

SANTA BARBARA

Resembling the palace of a prelate, the rambling Spanish-style courthouse has been described as the most beautiful civic building in the country. The structure overwhelms the viewer with the boldness of its proportions and the richness of its ornamentation. Everything about it is on a lavish scale: the decorated walls of the central hall rise several stories to a frescoed ceiling; richly patterned wrought ironwork carries the Spanish motif to every corner of the great building.

150

151

SANTA BARBARA

*The tradition-minded city displays its appreciation of the Spanish heritage
in various ways. Shoppers stroll through a pleasant shaded street of
Spanish-style stores, which front on a flagstone passageway as narrow as a
village street in Spain. During the three nights of the full moon in August,
residents celebrate a re-creation of the old Spanish days. Costumed horsemen
on richly caparisoned Palominos from nearby ranches ride in the colorful
parade that is the main feature of the festival.*

SANTA BARBARA

The beautiful façade of the Queen of the Missions, catching the light of early morning, stands as an impressive monument to the devotion, skill, and energy of the handful of padres who were able to create the massive structure in 1815 from simple materials at hand, with few tools, and with the help of unskilled Indians. The blend of Spanish–Moorish architecture is graced by the classic façade, derived from a design in a 1st century book on architecture written by a Roman scholar.

Martin Litton

SANTA BARBARA

A mule-drawn wagon and its duplicate shadow totes supplies to a ranch crew working far beyond the end of the road. The afternoon sun casts long shadows over the quiet hills of San Marcos Pass, gateway to the far-flung ranch country behind Santa Barbara. In the green, oak-grown hills, horses graze in the open pastures; and dairy herds, following the contours of the slopes as they forage, wear corduroy-striped patterns into the grassy hillsides.

157

The South Coast

For those who enjoy beach living, either as resident or visitor, the South Coastal area running from Ventura to San Juan Capistrano offers a rich concentration of aquatic sights and experiences.

For many miles, the coastal shelf slopes so gradually into the sea that the wide expanses of sandy beach slow the rolling surf to a gentle, lacy swirl. Cliffs and rocks are in abundance, but they do not dominate the shoreline, and the miles of open strand are easily accessible. A warm ocean current, running south from Point Conception, tempers the surf to an agreeable mildness; and though fogs and mist occasionally roll in off the ocean, the sky is usually clear and the salty air is soft and balmy.

The coastal strip offers a variety of scenic vistas. At its northern end, a forest of derricks stands in the pounding surf, serenely pumping oil from deep in the earth, oblivious to the surge of the tides. A wide highway sweeps along the shore almost at sea level, running a gauntlet between the thundering surf and tall cliffs that seem to teeter overhead. All along the way, homes are built as close to the sea as possible, some on the sand just beyond the reach of the highest tide and some on the bluffs above, jumbled closely together, each seeking the most advantageous view of the Pacific. In the sheltered channels offshore, small boats trace busy patterns in the blue water that separates the mainland from a scattering of island beach colonies.

An arid land, its open hills and fields are either matted with chaparral or covered with wild grass that is scorched brown in summer. Most of the verdure has been introduced by man. The headlands and inland valleys are greened over with irrigated fields of beans, tomatoes, and alfalfa, boxed-in by tall eucalyptus windbreaks. In the beach towns, files of spindly, mop-headed palms rise into the sky, marking the course of the streets or the presence of a shopping center. The gardens glow with subtropical blossoms set off by large-leafed shrubs; and here and there, flashes of incandescent magenta and pink signal the presence of bougainvillea or ice plant, whose intense colors rival the brilliance of the sun.

158

ef Muench

David Muench

159

Josef Muench

South Coast

Oil is where you find it—even under the ocean. The venturesome derricks march out into the breakers and draw black gold from deep in the earth beneath the sea's edge. In the late afternoon sun, the spidery rigs take on an air of fragility in contrast to the surging surf and the crude cliffs. The black, oil-stained derricks stand out starkly against the frothy white breakers that swirl through a forest of piling and spend themselves on the smooth beach.

SOUTH COAST

The moods of the ocean change from hour to hour. Under the light of a full moon, Laguna Beach takes on an air of romance, of mystery and of foreboding. The muted thunder of the breakers speaks to thoughtful man of sheathed power, of the infinity of water stretching across the world, and of the mystery of life's beginnings. In a different mood, the waves of daytime challenge the man of action to pit his skills against the denizens of the tides and to taste the dangers of the smashing surf.

SOUTH COAST

The white surf rolls gently up the wide, crescent beach at Malibu and stops far short of the homes built beyond the reach of the high, high tide. Children explore the spume-flecked sands, collecting the treasures of the sea. Farther down the coastline at Pacific Palisades, Mediterranean-style homes cling to the bluffs, overlooking the sea and the rugged promontories. Below them, between the cliffs and the pounding surf, a broad highway follows the jagged shoreline into the hazy distance.

SOUTH COAST

*Unfettered by tradition, the southern Californian freely seeks fresh solutions
to standard problems. The unique little Wayfarers' Chapel by Lloyd
Wright, built on a promontory in Palos Verdes, welcomes all faiths to
meditate and worship within its luminous walls of glass. The
aspirations of a community are symbolized in the striking design of Santa
Monica's civic auditorium, whose flying buttresses leap skyward.*

167

SOUTH COAST

*Small boats gather in orderly
ranks in Avalon Bay, the beautiful
harbor of Santa Catalina Island.
Behind them looms the matronly
form of the S. S. Catalina, a spic-
and-span vessel that has been
ferrying tourists to and from the
mainland since 1924. The
chaparral-covered hills, rising
steeply from the bay, are built-up
with Spanish-style homes, resorts,
and stores. A naturally rocky and
arid island, Catalina has been
fashioned into an attractive resort
with landscaped gardens, parks,
and groves of tropical trees.*

168

SOUTH COAST

*The stately ruins of Mission San Juan Capistrano seem to echo to the ghostly
footfalls of the padres and Indians who worshipped and labored here for
the brief years of its life. One of the most beautiful of the California chain, the
massive structure was largely destroyed by an earthquake in 1812, a scant
six years after its completion. It has never completely recovered. The
standing arcades still show the scars of the quake. Only unscathed link with
the past is the richly ornamented, gold-leafed altar.*

Los Angeles

The great, sprawling city of Los Angeles spreads over a dry alluvial plain that fans out from the base of the mountains and runs to the sea. Naturally flat, the site offers few elevated vantage points and little relief from the grand monotony of its sweep. Here and there a chain of hills plows into the sea of buildings, or a wooded, dry watercourse meanders through, but in general the structural ocean spreads without hindrance or relief in all directions.

Viewed from above, this prairie of buildings takes on an amazing transformation. A raw, pulsing vitality seems to rise from the massed structures. The audacious freeways flow through the city, weaving, crossing, and blending together like themes in a musical score. From the heights, even the smog acquires a perverse beauty as it veils parts of the city from sight. At night, the horizonless sweep of the lights outshines the starlit heavens with its geometric constellations and clusters of auroral color where the neon gathers.

Most of the elements of grace and beauty within the city are man-made and are scattered over a broad canvas. Sylvan parks, graced with lakes and bright subtropical plantings, landscaped grounds of museums and art galleries, and verdant campuses bring oases of graceful verdure into the heart of the metropolis.

Architecturally, the city displays a venturesome creativity that adds luster to the prospect. Hillside and canyon residential areas reveal progressive and imaginative home designs and landscaping practices. Broad boulevards, most notably Wilshire, run for miles through canyons of fresh, attractive business structures designed with taste and restraint.

The influence of Hollywood may show up here and there in flamboyant night club and restaurant façades, but at its best, it produces delightful surprises, such as the bits of Disneyland that charm the eye with flashes of nostalgic beauty.

Like most of Southern California, Los Angeles is more interested in today than yesterday, and the picturesque relics of its colorful history are nearly submerged in the metropolitan sweep. However, two imposing missions, a restoration of the original Spanish plaza, and a scattering of fine museums provide an illuminating glimpse into the city's heritage.

On the outskirts of the city, a mountain playground swings around the northeastern periphery and a lively water-world along the western edge. Both of these are treated in separate chapters.

Richard Dawson

David Muench

William Aplin

Los Angeles (Following Page)   © William A. Garnett

One of the most extraordinary sights in all California is the view of Los Angeles from an airplane. An ocean of buildings runs from the mountains to the sea in a vast mirage. The sight of the massed humanity spread out over the open miles below overwhelms the viewer with an awareness of the immense vitality and power of this unusual city.

173

Pete Andreadis

LOS ANGELES

From the heights, the great Los Angeles basin presents a fascinating and changeable spectacle. At night, the myriads of sparkling lights cluster together in rectangular formations that appear from Griffith Park like an orderly reflection of the starry sky itself. In the daytime, under the dour spell of a heavy smog, the dimming city takes on an air of somber beauty.

LOS ANGELES
Great traffic arteries carry the life blood of the sprawling city from its heart
to its farthest extremities. At night, the freeways become rivers of light,
criss-crossing high above the business district. In the light of day, the
Gargantuan sweep of the major roadways is breath-taking in its audacity.
The broad channel of Harbor Freeway carries a pulsing flow of tens of
thousands of vehicles to and from the business core of the city.

David Muench

LOS ANGELES
Extremes in architectural statement: gilded convolutions of the elevator court of the old Bradbury Building (1893); and the rhythmic repetitions of latterday Wilshire Boulevard façades.

185

LOS ANGELES

In a pleasant sylvan setting, the oily waters of Hancock Park mirror the clean white expanse of an office building (1948 A.D.) and the plaster shapes of prehistoric beasts (14,000 B.C.) that were drawn to their deaths in a treacherous, tarry bog under the placid surface of the pond. Of a far different complexion, MacArthur Park offers a shady oasis on the outer edge of the downtown area. The palm-fringed lake is often dotted with small boats, poking leisurely about under battery power.

186

Union Pacific Railroad

187

William Aplin

Los Angeles

West Los Angeles is a showcase of fresh and imaginative commercial development. Wide Wilshire Boulevard conveys an impression of uncrowded spaciousness, despite the prodigious volume of traffic and the intensive use of the buildings on either side, because of the discreet handling of off-street parking, the wide spacing of the buildings, and the airy treatment of the ground floor of the newer buildings, invitingly landscaped with gardens, pools, and arcades. The cylindrical Capitol Records building, especially appropriate to the business it houses, brings a bold architectural statement to Hollywood.

188

LOS ANGELES
Hollywood Freeway soars over the city bearing its name and snakes through the rumpled Santa Monica Mountains to reach the spreading carpet of homes in San Fernando Valley.

190

Los Angeles

*At night, the strains of classical music float over the hills of Hollywood
from the great shell in Hollywood Bowl. An audience of 20,000 music-lovers
sits in rapt attention in the balmy air, absorbed in the "Symphony Under
the Stars." In the background, traffic courses over a freeway, lights twinkle
in the hillside homes, and the Los Angeles basin glows with star-spangled
activity. In the light of day, beauty visits the hills in a different guise. Not
far away, the muscular curve of Hollywood Dam restrains a placid lake,
shimmering in the noontime sun.*

Gene Stein

LOS ANGELES

The giant, landscaped campus of the University of California at Los Angeles (20,000 students) spreads over 465 acres of terraced foothills off Sunset Boulevard, next to Westwood Village. Imposing, brick-walled, tile-roofed buildings of Romanesque design face each other across a broad esplanade in the center of the campus.

194

LOS ANGELES (FOLLOWING PAGE)   *John S. Weir and Henry T. Conserva*

The simple dignity of old Spanish architecture and the peacefulness of venerable age combine to give the San Fernando Mission an atmosphere of quiet charm. The cool, musty interior of the chapel reveals the primitive touch of the native craftsmen who naively blended pagan and Christian motifs in their decorations. Founded in 1797, the mission prospered for forty years and then fell into disuse for a century. It is being conscientiously and systematically restored to its original form.

195

LOS ANGELES AREA

*Scores of fanciful and elaborate floats, fashioned of thousands of roses,
orchids, and carnations, move sedately down canopied Colorado Boulevard
between thick walls of spectators in Pasadena's annual Tournament of Roses.
After the parade, the festivities shift to the Rose Bowl for the New Year's
Day football classic, pioneer of the post-season contests (started in 1916).
The huge bowl stands on the outskirts of the city in Brookside Park, flanked
on both sides by wooded residential areas graced with fine homes and
beautiful gardens.*

William Aplin

Los Angeles Area

The white marble Huntington Art Gallery stands in classic repose in the midst of immaculately groomed, formal gardens. The aloof dignity of the pillared façade proclaims the importance of the building's mission to preserve the priceless artwork of the past. Not far away, a different kind of museum peers through tall palms fringing a lagoon at the County Arboretum. The filigreed cottage, built in 1881 by a mining millionaire for his bride, is used as an historical museum.

200

David Muench

LOS ANGELES AREA

Ornamental iron gates swing wide to welcome the meditative visitor to the peaceful courtyard of Mission San Gabriel (1806). The arched adobe gateway reflects in the tranquil old fountain and the rainwater collected on the worn brick paving. Inside the church, a richly decorated altar glows in the muted light. Painted and gilded figures of the Saints, elaborate scrolls, and other religious ornaments show the firm but unschooled hand of the Indian craftsmen who fashioned them a century and a half ago.

LOS ANGELES AREA

The labyrinthine, Spanish-style Mission Inn in Riverside offers the visitor a rare opportunity to immerse himself in the rich artistic heritage of the early Spanish-Mexican settlers. Two stories of guest rooms look down upon a gallery containing old Spanish and Mexican paintings and furnishings. The Atrio of St. Francis, paved with vari-colored travertine, resembles a courtyard of an old city in Spain, with its shrines and bronze fountain.

LOS ANGELES AREA

The richly exciting symbols of the vigorous past turn up at Disneyland in delightful form. The pinnacled castle of Sleeping Beauty is at once droll and appropriately menacing. The bastion seems to echo to the clank of armor, the sighs of imprisoned maidens, and the snorts of circling dragons. The elegantly trimmed river boat, replica of an extinct species of proud and handsome vessels, churns its nostalgic way through the 1890's, in waters infested with hypothetical alligators.

207

San Diego

Blessed by a genial climate that encourages outdoor living all through the year, San Diegans concentrate with enthusiasm on the enjoyment of an idyllic water-world that embraces a magnificent landlocked harbor and a limitless strand of silvery beaches.

The quiet waters of the bay, protected from the ocean's surges by natural breakwaters, provides shelter for a melange of vessels of all sizes and shapes. Hosts of small pleasure craft cut frisky wakes among the monsters of ocean commerce and a conglomeration of dark gray navy ships anchored in the bay or cruising majestically through the blue water. Along the bayshore, hundreds of moth-balled fighting ships are moored together in tight packs, hull to hull.

Along the ocean shore, a series of white bathing beaches runs for 30-odd miles from Del Mar almost to the Mexican border. Here, under the ever-azure sky, thousands of swimmers come to ride the tepid breakers or to sun on the sand. In Mission Bay Park—an immense inland extension of the ocean playground—waterskiers, multicolored sails, and excursion boats pass to and fro in a lively minuet.

Not all of it open beach, the coastline presents a variety of scenic sights. The intricate, lacy patterns eroded into the cliffs of Torrey Pines Mesa look like giant shawls dropping down into the water. At La Jolla, the surf swirls among the rocks of a sheltered bathing cove; and at high-high tide, the breakers smash against the cliffs in towering explosions of spray. Farther south, the long, high promontory of Point Loma stretches a protecting arm across the entrance to the bay and offers from its heights an unequaled view of the city and the shimmering Pacific.

A very different kind of attraction, verdant Balboa Park spreads its 1,400 acres of landscaped arroyos and mesas in a veritable Forest of Arden in the heart of the city. Some of the old rococo buildings of the exposition of 1915 still stand amid immaculately kept grounds, shaded by tall, blue-green eucalyptus trees. Not the least of the park's attractions is the picturesque zoo, where the denizens prowl in natural grottoes.

A pastoral, unspoiled back country lies to the east of the city. The old Mission, first in the California chain (1774), stands in dignified decay in a quiet valley. Beyond, a series of farming valleys recedes to the east, giving way eventually to pine-shadowed mountains that drop off abruptly to the silvery sink of the Imperial Valley a mile straight down.

208

William Reid

209

William Reid

Union Tribune Publishing Company

SAN DIEGO

The cage-like lantern room of the Old Spanish Lighthouse (1855) on the tip of Point Loma offers a breathtaking full-circle view of the San Diego area. Far below spreads the busy bay, landlocked by Coronado and North Island, with its armada of grim, gray war vessels and frivolous little pleasure craft mingling on the sheltered water. Beyond, the chalky buildings of San Diego ascend the slope of a natural amphitheater and recede into the purple hills. Off the tip of Point Loma, white sails speckle the open sea as a flotilla of yachts weighs anchor for a race to Acapulco.

SAN DIEGO

*The richly ornamented, Spanish-style buildings of Balboa Park, in their
neatly landscaped setting, form an oasis of beauty in the heart of San Diego.
The airy crowns of tall eucalyptus trees float high above the buildings, almost
matching the height of the beautiful California Tower, which looms in the
background. San Diegans have taken proud delight in the rococo detailing,
long shaded arcades, and luxuriant semi-tropical gardens of the park ever
since it was first opened for the exposition of 1915.*

William Reid

SAN DIEGO

One of the most striking features of Balboa Park is the massive
Botanical Building, where luxuriant tropical plants thrive under
an arching sky of wooden lath. Of less impersonal moment is the
children's zoo, where the denizens can be met first-hand, and where
ridiculous birds can be fed peanuts by solemn little girls.

Ernest Braun

SAN DIEGO

Of the few visible reminders of the city's Spanish past, the one that most vividly recreates the hospitable atmosphere of those leisurely years is Ramona's Marriage Place (1825), with its inviting, shady corredor *enclosing a colorful garden. The plain façade of the San Diego Mission shows the strain of the years; yet with all its cracked plaster and eroded adobe, it wears an air of simple dignity. First (1774) in the chain of the California missions, it has lived a long and arduous existence. After decades of neglect and vandalism, it has been only partially restored.*

216

217

SAN DIEGO

The noble old Hotel Del Coronado, one of the few luxury resorts in California remaining from the 1890's, carries forward a tradition of impeccable service in opulent surroundings. The immaculate white structure, with its red turrets and cupolas and hundreds of windows, conjures visions of visiting royalty and Presidents, of varnished hacks rolling under the porte cochère, of grand balls in the high-vaulted Crown Room under the great crystal chandeliers. An island of traditional service in the modern day, it represents a marked contrast to the relaxed atmosphere of the attractive new resorts along Mission Bay, with their playful architecture and shoreside accommodations.

218

Roy Krell

Josef Muench

SAN DIEGO

*Towering waves explode against the sandstone cliffs of La Jolla in a
spectacular display of awesome power. The scouring waves slice and pockmark
the face of the bluffs where they expose layers and pockets of soft rock. High
above the battleworn cliffs stand the homes and apartments of the town,
their windows faced towards the dramatic arena below.*

Edward Sievers

San Diego

Serene and silent, four gliders soar like eagles on the rising air columns off the cliffs of Torrey Pines Mesa. The steady flow of air that supports the pilots in their free flight also torments the plant materials that grow along the brow of the cliffs. The forceful winds cause the pines for whom the mesa is named to grow into forms of grotesque beauty, their twisted branches seeming to ward off the unrelenting wind.

222

Josef Muench

SAN DIEGO

In a pleasant little valley, the red and white San Luis Rey Mission (completed 1802) reposes in the afternoon sun. The bronze bells in the campanario no longer summon hundreds of Luiseño Indians to worship or to work. In its prime, it was the largest mission in the chain, and its buildings ranged over six and a half acres. All that now remains of much of the original cloisters is a procession of plastered adobe arches, vaguely reminiscent of an ancient Roman aqueduct.

William Aplin

SAN DIEGO

The road that ascends the flank of Mount Palomar offers a sweeping panorama of green valleys and rows of tumbled mountain ranges, receding into the misty horizon. On Palomar's summit, the helmet-like dome of the 200-inch telescope looms incongruously above the pines and oaks.

226

The Desert

The desert casts a spell over all who know it well. A strange and lonely land, a place of mystery and of violent extremes, of serenity and stillness, it exerts a hypnotic pull that draws men to its haunting beauty.

In its natural state, the desert stretches in seeming emptiness to the far, purple hills in a shimmering vista of great serenity. Around its horizons run the bare, treeless mountains, stripped to the naked earth by abrasive winds and flash floods. The exposed soil reveals itself in bizarre reds, browns, blacks, and yellows that become transformed by the haze of distance into magenta, blues, and purples. The eroded mountains, boldly sculptured by the cutting wind and water, present stark shadow patterns in the slanting rays of morning or late afternoon.

At the base of the richly colored hills spreads a treeless plain of sandy gravel or an ocean of sand dunes, raked by the wind into frozen wave patterns. Low, gray creosote bushes dot the high desert area, interspersed with prickly cactus plants of an enchanting virtuosity of form or the disjointed figures of Joshua trees spaced out over the plain.

In the raw desert, the handiwork of man is seldom apparent. No windbreaks limit the horizon, no farmhouses or windmills catch the eye, no crops cover the land. The feeling of isolation is intensified by the profound stillness that makes even the littlest sound seem important—the faint scrabbling of a lizard or a bird in the dry scrub, the whisper of a warm breeze that comes from nowhere and goes nowhere.

The desert reveals the arrival of spring long before the rest of the state awakens. A carpet of lavender sand verbena colors the sandy washes, orange poppies flame over the hills of the Mojave, and tamarisks open like puffs of pink smoke. The whiplike ocotillos burst out with bright red fringes, yuccas hold their snowy plumes aloft, and the cacti display exquisitely formed, waxy flowers. The show does not last long—for summer also comes early and turns its unrelenting heat upon the plants.

The desert is unforgiving to those who break its rules, but men have learned to tame its harshness and to put the land to practical uses. Thousands of acres of wasteland have been reclaimed by irrigation and the fertile sandy soil made to burgeon forth with bumper crops of cotton, melons, and lettuce. In the towns, vacation colonies, and resorts that are scattered throughout, residents live the year around in air-conditioned comfort, and vacationers flock to the resorts to soak up the warm winter sun.

John Robinson

Union Pacific Railroad

William Aplin

229

William A. Garnett, courtesy Bank of America N.T. & S.A.

THE DESERT

*An irrigation canal zigzags across the floor of the
desert, transforming the sandy wastes into neatly
engraved acres of row-crops and regiments of fruit trees.
Around the edges, the dead wrinkled mountains stand,
gaunt reminders of what was—and what might be
again if the water ever stopped flowing in the big canal.*

231

THE DESERT

In its natural abundance, the desert blossoms forth in rich variety. Tough, wiry plants, uniquely adapted to thin soil, searing sun, and lack of rain, thrive on the arid wastes of the Mojave and Colorado Deserts. Shaggy, contorted Joshua trees stand silhouetted against rocky hills in the first light of dawn. Spring comes in a pastel wash of evening primrose and sand verbena, spread over the dunes, or in the spectacular show of the plumed Yuccas, holding their snowy flames high above the desert scrub.

Josef Muench

233

The Desert

The deadly beauty of the desert is nowhere more discernible than in the wastes where neither plant nor animal can live. Riffled sand flows to the far horizon in waves of wind-smoothed dunes, lonely, hostile, and hauntingly beautiful. In the Death Valley sink, the icy crests of the Panamints reflect unblemished in the still water of a poisonous, alkaline pool.

The Desert (Overleaf)

Ansel Adams

The jumbled mountains of Death Valley, striped with barbaric reds and browns, yellows and greens, take on a lunar look under a glowering sky.

The Southern Mountains

Around the inland edges of the Los Angeles plain looms a vast amphitheater of mountains, composed of a series of ranges bearing musical Spanish names—the Santa Monicas, San Gabriels, San Jacintos, and Santa Anas—and offering from their crests some of the most unusual visual contrasts in California.

The mountains rise abruptly from near sea level and ascend several thousand feet, reaching a climax in four towering peaks that are more than 10,000 feet in height. Dry and barren on their lower slopes, they turn green as the altitude increases and reach a forested crest, set with mile-high lakes.

The traveler winding his way up the grades runs in a few miles through a succession of life zones equivalent to a trip from Mexico to northern Canada. In short order, he passes from palms and cactus through hills mantled with chaparral, thence into forests of ponderosa pine, incense cedar, and fir, and finally emerges in an alpine setting of lichens and mosses, far above timberline. From a wooded crest, he can look down to the silvery desert, simmering in the heat 8,000 feet below.

Easily accessible, the ranges are broached by broad, double-track freeways that climb in bold sweeps through wide, open passes and give access to slow-paced highways that twist their way up the canyons to reach the sparkling lakes and shady, resinous forests of the upper elevations. Many of the drives are notable scenic experiences in themselves: the Rim-of-the-World Drive, Angeles Crest Highway, and Palms-to-Pines Highway disclose frequent vistas of breathtaking scope—views of sharply eroded desert hills of red and purple, of wooded slopes jumbled together in ascending ridges, or of the incredible metropolitan sweep, especially sensational after dark when the twinkling cities light the black plain as far as the eye can see.

The march of the seasons draws the Angeleno to the heights to enjoy the changes that are barely perceptible in the mild climate of the lowlands. In spring, wildflowers and blossoming shrubs brighten the lower slopes with a colorful tide that slowly advances up the mountainsides as the season moves into summer. The rainless months cast a hot, dusty spell over the forests that lasts until the relief of the first fall storms, which rinse the boughs, soak the needle-carpeted soil, and fill the air with a bracing fragrance. Autumn flashes briefly and gives way quickly to winter, signaled by heavy snowfall in the higher elevations. People throng to the winter playgrounds to ski or toboggan; many come to enjoy their very first contact with snow, and some come to marvel at the sight of the warm desert basking in the sun far below while they stand mufflered, mittened, and shivering on the top of the world.

Val Samuelson

David Muench

Horst Ahlberg

239

SOUTHERN MOUNTAINS
Below the viewer on top of Mount Wilson spreads a checkerboard plain, cut by a wandering seasonal river and bordered by the Santa Ana Mountains, climaxed by Mt. Estelle beneath the eagle-shaped clouds. A far more awesome sight can be seen at night, when the telescopes in the silvery buildings are trained on the stars.

SOUTHERN MOUNTAINS

The southern mountains offer surprising extremes within a span of a few miles. Cajon Pass, snaking its way through the San Gabriel Mountains on its way to the desert, runs for miles through dry, gray, sage-covered ranges. Always in sight, the snow-dusted, 10,000-foot hump of Old Baldy towers on the horizon. On the other side of the snowy crest lies a highly developed winter sports area, where skiers can schuss their way among the crystalline trees in a setting of tingling purity.

Victor Stein

SOUTHERN MOUNTAINS

In a scene of snowy tranquility, winter transforms Lake Arrowhead Village into a Swiss Christmas card. Thick snow clings to the roofs of the chalets, drips off the eaves in glistening icicles, and chokes the streets in massive drifts. It is hard to believe that this nostalgic sight is less than three hours away from balmy Los Angeles! In another season, the pine-rimmed lake appears in a different guise, as it reflects the summer sun in its spangled surface.

SOUTHERN MOUNTAINS

The water ripples gently, invitingly, around rocky Treasure Island in Big Bear Lake. Though a resort area, its many cabins and camps are barely visible in the open forest. On Lake Arrowhead, sailboats skim over the wavelets and powerboats wait at the pier for the yank of the starting lanyard.

Lake Arrowhead Division

Horst Ahlberg

247

The Sierra Nevada

No one who has ever watched the alpenglow on Half Dome fade into forgetfulness, or seen puffy white clouds scudding across Lake Tahoe, driven by winds that roar through the treetops like freight trains crossing a trestle, or who has stood in reverent awe in the presence of the Giant Sequoias can ever forget the majestic world of the Sierra Nevada.

Within the boundaries of this granite domain are countless visual experiences that linger in the memory. Rivers foaming over rocky beds in the full tide of spring, or gently meandering along in the last leisurely trickle of fall. Waterfalls that drop hundreds of feet in a gauzy torrent that shakes the ground with the force of the falling tons of water; or gentler falls that cascade down in a veiled mist that captures the rainbow in its spray. Rocky, conifer-rimmed lakes that sparkle in the morning sun, as the breezes chase each other across the smooth surface, or turn to choppy gray in the afternoon when the wind churns the surface into whitecaps that slam against the boats that drone across the troubled water. Quiet meadows, dressed with blue lupine or yellow monkey flowers, where deer graze and an occasional bear shuffles across, following a favorite path.

Crystal-clear nights that seem to reveal more stars than ever existed before. Brief, violent electrical storms that smash against the granite peaks, echoing and re-echoing in wild counterpoint, and then move on, grumbling, to cannonade some distant range.

The bright splash of autumn, changing the tall trees to pillars of orange, scarlet, and yellow that slowly shed their saucer-size leaves in graceful showers. And finally, the white blanket of winter that seals the high passes, calls out the skier to test the powdery snow, and settles a pure crystalline stillness over the frosted land.

The enumeration could be continued indefinitely without exhausting the memorable features of the Sierra. It is sights and experiences such as these that reward those who come to the Sierra, no matter how briefly, with physical renewal and spiritual refreshment.

The Sierra Nevada (Spanish for "snowy range") has been authoritatively defined as "the longest, highest, and the grandest single mountain range in the United States." Rising gradually in the west to its 7,000 to 14,000-foot crest, the range drops off abruptly to the east into a long desert-like trough. The majestic mountain complex runs nearly 400 miles along the backbone of the state, from Lake Tahoe to Walker Pass. A special province within the Sierra is the "High Country," a serene and separate world, which is visited in the next chapter.

SIERRA NEVADA

East of the Sierra and across the Owens Valley, a storm lifts from the Inyo Mountains, leaving a light dusting of early snow. The gnome-like rocks of the Alabama Hills in the foreground, some as large as five-story buildings, are thought to be the oldest rock formation on this continent.

SIERRA NEVADA (OVERLEAF)

Dawn bathes the jagged, snow-covered scarp of the Sierra Nevada in radiant light, while the low hills still slumber under the spell of night.

Ansel Adams

250

Powell and Edna Jenkins

251

Theodore Osmundson

SIERRA NEVADA

*A peaceful lake in the Mammoth area lies cupped in a tranquil basin,
rimmed by forests of hemlock and fir and enclosed by the looming wall of
the Sierra escarpment. Near timberline, the surrounding mountains are
covered with alternating swaths of forest and talus slides of naked granite.
Over the hump of the Sierra and down at the foot of a rough, winding road,
the Devils Postpile presents a fascinating spectacle of massed basaltic
prisms, looking like a gigantic magnification of some microscopic form of
pure crystalline structure.*

Ray Atkeson

256

Frances Coleberd

SIERRA NEVADA

*Justly regarded as one of the State's most beautiful sights,
Lake Tahoe rewards the viewer with breathtaking vistas.
Encircling pine forests provide a setting of green velvet for
jewel-like Emerald Bay, and beyond the gap in the forest,
the shimmering reaches of the azure lake stretch to the Nevada
mountains. On a wintry day, the jumbled rocks of Rubicon
Point stand silhouetted against gathering thunderheads, and
the water stirs restlessly in the presence of the coming storm.*

257

SIERRA NEVADA

As the early morning sun casts long shadows down the white mountainsides, a lone skier leaves the warmth of a snow-roofed cabin to try his skill on the powdery runs of Squaw Mountain. Skiers flash down a long slope, scribing fresh doodles into the pure white surface. At the head of the chairlift, the interwoven ski tracks have carved the snow into a gray-white brocade.

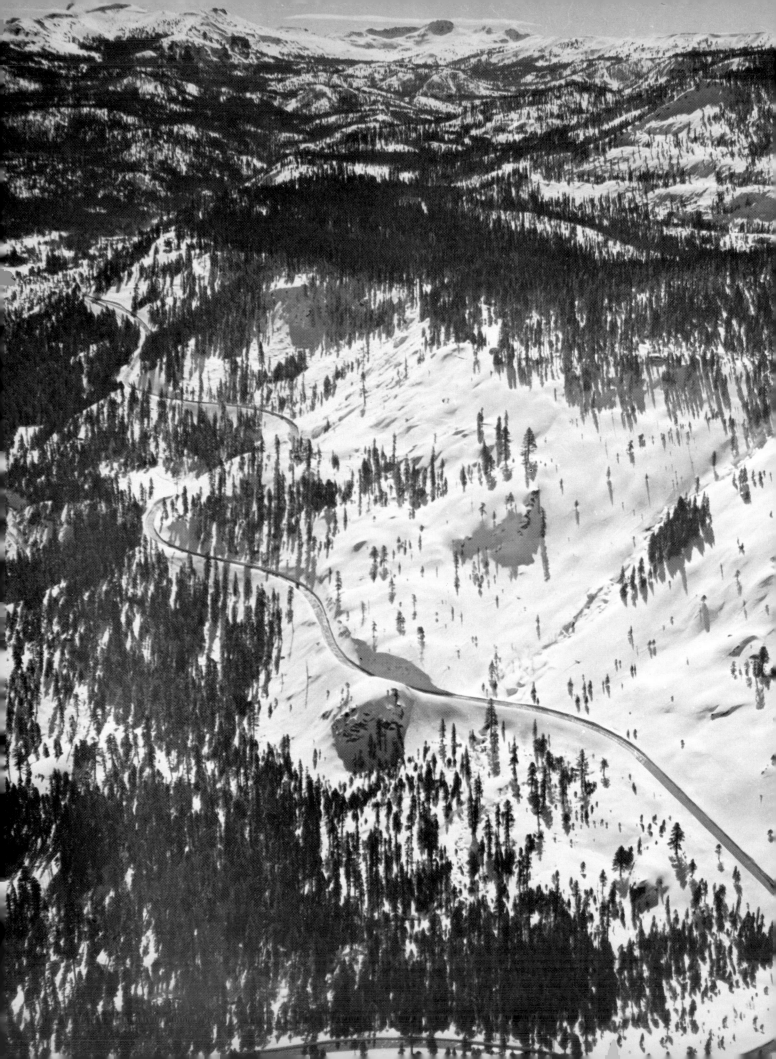

SIERRA NEVADA

*Heavy snows fall on the Sierra, mantling the forests, meadows, and roads
in a deep impenetrable quilt of glistening white. The little-traveled roads
remain covered until the sun finds them in the spring, but the through
highways are kept open by giant snowplows. Traffic flows unabated along
Meyers Grade that snakes down from Echo Summit; Gargantuan diesel
tankers, exhaling plumes of steamy smoke, rumble up the cleared passes beside
tall, menacing cliffs of snow.*

Richard Dawson

SIERRA NEVADA

For more than a century, Californians have thrilled to the dramatic grandeur of Yosemite's domes, waterfalls, and incomparable vistas. The Old Village Chapel, built in 1879, still serves worshipers and wedding parties, as it has done for three generations. Under a fresh fall of snow, the quaint little chapel looks like a page from a New England calendar. Not far away, across a grassy meadow, Yosemite Falls drop down the opposite wall of the valley. A wispy trickle in winter, the falls thunder over the brink in the full tide of spring and cascade down the cliffs in an unbridled torrent.

SIERRA NEVADA (OVERLEAF)   Ansel Adams

Swirling masses of storm clouds, gathering on the rim of Yosemite Valley, amplify the majesty of the beautiful valley in a scene of Jovian splendor.

262

Richard Dawson

Sierra Nevada
Away from the crowds, the Valley is a quiet place, where deer splash across the river in peace and the oak leaves shimmer delicately in the breeze against a backdrop of eternal granite.

266

SIERRA NEVADA
In the light of early morning, the motionless surface of Mirror Lake duplicates the surrounding mountains with crystal clarity in a setting of majestic repose.

268

Ansel Adams

Sierra Nevada

*Few sights are more overwhelming than the view from the tip of Glacier
Point, whether it be snow-capped Half Dome looming above the clouds or the
spring rush of the snow-melt over the faraway falls of the Merced River.*

270

SIERRA NEVADA

The massive granite bulk of Moro Rock in Sequoia National Park soars to a top-of-the-world outlook, where an awesome, full-circle panorama, ranging from the Central Valley to the High Sierra, unrolls before the eye. Elsewhere in the Park, the Generals Highway runs through airy groves of giant Sierra redwoods, tall sturdy trees whose heavy trunks and muscular branches have withstood the onslaughts of fire, lightning, and crushing snow for two thousand years.

The High Country

In a *Sunset Book* about the national parks in California, Dorr Yeager, a noted outdoorsman and interpreter of nature subjects, eloquently summarizes the appeal of the High Country. He writes:

"It is not easy to describe the High Country, for such a description must encompass the five senses.

"It is not enough to describe what one sees—the peaks, gray at midday, pink with early morning and evening glow, and silhouetted against a star-studded sky at night; the unending miles of granite above timberline, with a hundred lakes glistening in the glacial-carved depressions; the high passes, snow-choked until midsummer and defying access to all but the birds and the winds; the birthplace of streams in high boggy meadows ablaze with bloom; and the streams themselves, noisy in their impatience to join the main river.

"Nor is it enough to describe the sounds—the chattering of a pine squirrel or the whistling of a marmot; the metallic ring of a boulder as it breaks from its place of origin to bounce down over the granite, or the deeper roar of a full-scale rock avalanche; the far scream of a hawk as it circles overhead; the tinkle of a rivulet; the splash of a leaping trout in some quiet lake; the stillness which is no sound at all but which at times pervades the High Country.

"Nor can odors be ignored, for who can forget the smell of a mountain morning —the pungence of pine needles in the heat of midday; the freshness that follows an afternoon shower; the odor of wood smoke at twilight. And the feel—of a mountain breeze; the warmth of sun by day and of campfire by night; the softness of a wooded trail under foot. Even taste, for there is nothing to compare with trout fried over an open fire, of biscuits baked in a reflector oven, or of beans baked in an iron pot deep in the coals. These things are all part of the mountain experience and no experience would be complete without them."

The land of which he writes is a unique subprovince of the Sierra Nevada, lying above timberline on the spine of the Sierra escarpment. Crossed by only one highway pass, it is trail country that can only be explored by foot or on horseback. The visitor carries his room and board in his pack and eats and sleeps in the open, on the roof of California.

Martin Litton

SIERRA NEVADA

*Here is the High Country—the Land of High Adventure—
John Muir's "Range of Light." But so vast is the sweep of
this tumbled wilderness that even an aerial view encompasses
a mere sampling. In this panorama, the terrain ranges from
Mounts Williamson and Whitney on the left horizon to
Kaweah Peaks Ridge on the right and sweeps down to the Rae
Lakes in the left foreground. The John Muir Trail zigzags
through this shining land, starting at Mount Whitney,
wandering off to the right, then swinging left to leave the
picture at Rae Lakes.*

SIERRA NEVADA
*The John Muir Trail
winds along the crest of
the Sierra in a lofty
wilderness uncrossed by
any road. Over the years,
the passage of thousands
of boots and hooves along
the trail has worn a
furrow in the high
meadows, such as this one
below Pinchot Pass.*

279

THE HIGH COUNTRY

*In the High Sierra, no roads mar the meadows, the white sandy "shores,"
or the sparse forests of scattered foxtail pine. From the summit of 11,000-foot
Cottonwood Pass, one of the gateways to the High Country from the Owens
Lake area, you look across the gentle Kern Plateau to the snow-spotted
spurs of the Great Western Divide beyond the unseen glacial canyon of the
Kern River. Farther to the north the summit of Mount Whitney (14,495
feet), king peak of the Sierra system, reveals a majestic panorama of
glacier-sculptured peaks and chasms.*

281

The Gold Country

For ten tumultuous years, an army of a quarter of a million young fortune-seekers turned a strip of the California foothills upside down in an epidemic quest for gold. The land that they worked over has never been the same since—nor for that matter has the state of California, which was catapulted from a lazy Spanish outpost to a full-fledged state of the Union by the impact of this explosive invasion.

The foothill area that the miners assaulted rolls pleasantly over the lower western slopes of the Sierra Nevada. Part-way between valley and mountain, it is a transitional mixture of chaparral-covered hills, pine forests, and open grassy fields shaded by scattered oaks. High enough to feel the bite of the seasons, the countryside bursts out in riotous color in fall and blossoms forth in spring with bright carpets of wildflowers. In summer, the open hills bake in dry and dusty somnolence.

Into this pastoral wilderness, the Fortyniners burst with pick and goldpan. Almost immediately, they established settlements of varying permanence and repute and labeled them with preposterous names such as Bogus Thunder, Git-up-and-git, Gomorrah, Humbug, Bed Bug, and a hundred others. A rambunctious, hard-drinking and hard-living lot, the men led a toilsome life, most of them on the thin edge of hardship and privation. Robberies, murders, and hangings were not uncommon; and the wooden towns were frequently wiped out by fire. The cannier merchants and residents learned to protect themselves and their valuables by building stone structures with sheet-iron roofs and steel-shuttered doors and windows. Some of these buildings are still in use, but many of them are now eyeless and roofless shells.

The wild growth of the area ended almost as abruptly as it began, but so vigorous and widespread was the impact of the Gold Rush on this compact area that its imprint still shows more than a century later. The scattered relics are tantalizing to view and to explore. The ghostly presence of the miners seems everywhere, haunting the vine-grown ruins, the pathetic graveyards with the teetering headstones, and the windowless churches. The museums and restored towns (most notably Columbia) intensify an illusion that the vanished men have just left for a few days and will soon be back to resume their digging. It is not difficult to imagine them out there in the hot hills, drenched in sweat, pausing in their labors to listen to the insistent, head-drilling buzz of the cicada that fills the sage-scented air.

Martin Litton

283

GOLD COUNTRY

Every keyhole in every rusty iron door, every boarded-up hole and gaping doorframe is a window into the lusty past of the Gold Country. With pathetic grandeur, the staunch masonry walls stand in crumbling defiance of time, monuments to the optimism of long-forgotten Forty niners who built securely in a temporary world.

Richard Dawson

GOLD COUNTRY
Spare, white courthouses, hotels, and churches, carried here from New England in the minds of their builders, give a touch of settled dignity to the raw foothills of the Gold Country.

Clyde Childress

John Robinson

GOLD COUNTRY

In the high, wooded hills La Porte lies dozing in the hot, piney stillness of summer, dreaming, perhaps, of the days when it was a bustling, brawling center for hydraulic miners. A hundred years ago the miners turned their powerful nozzles on the mountains and washed out the gold hidden deep inside. In so doing, they reshaped the landscape and created such eerie sights as the Malakoff Diggings, where the exposed, multi-colored cliffs rise above milky-blue, man-made lakes.

288

GOLD COUNTRY

*The weathered old churches
with their poignant, weedy
graveyards seem to be waiting
for the return of the devout
miners who built them, filled
their pews, and sang in their
choir lofts a century ago—and
then suddenly moved on to
fairer lodes, abandoning the
chapels and headstones to the
mischief of sun, wind, frost.*

Martin Litton

GOLD COUNTRY

The elegant, wedding-cake design of the façade of old Firehouse No. 1 (now a museum) proudly proclaims its equality with the school, the church, and the courthouse as an institution of eminence in the Gold Country, where all that protected the tinder towns from occasional obliteration was an efficient fire department. Apparently, the firefighters of Nevada City did their job well, for this town, nestled in a bowl in the pine-clad mountains, has remained virtually unchanged since the 1850's, and its steep streets and well-preserved buildings transport the visitor back to Gold Rush days.

The Central Valley

Viewed from a vantage point on the mountains that encircle it, the great Central Valley presents a majestic and changeable panorama.

In the hard light of day, the level miles spread out in a giant's checkerboard, with squares of cultivated land—green orchards and leaf crops, golden wheat, or white cotton—alternating with rich brown acres of fallow soil. Tall windbreaks of cottonwoods and eucalyptus extend the lines of the checkerboard into the air. Lacing through the pattern, the tree-bordered rivers follow wandering courses and the glistening silver ribbons of the irrigation canals trace a zigzag path through the land. Here and there a small cluster of shade trees indicates the site of a ranch house, and a dense grove, the location of a crossroad settlement.

At dusk, when the Valley dims with haze and the checkered land recedes from view, the great sink begins to look like an inland sea contained between mountainous shores—as indeed it once was in the geologic past. After nightfall, an inky blackness steals over the land and the empty dark is broken only here and there by the lonely lights of a farmhouse, the twinkling nebulae of a distant city, and automobile headlights moving through the black like lazy fireflies.

Key to the fertility of the Valley's burgeoning acres is the river system, natural and man-made, that awakens the earth with the gift of water. The rivers bring a special way of life into the hot Valley. Nostalgic little towns dream on the wooded banks of the Sacramento, marking the spot where proud sternwheelers once stopped in the heyday of the river. Children swim in the swift currents or fish from leaky skiffs or the bascule bridges. In the crazy-quilt Delta, where the great rivers meet in a jigsaw puzzle of islets and tule-bordered channels, fishing boats poke about in persistent quest of "stripers."

Many of the Valley's cities and towns dating from Gold Rush days have a settled and prosperous air. Their well-kept old homes and shaded streets, canopied by great elms planted by the early settlers, present a picture of peaceful continuity. The spic-and-span relics of historical moment and the massive buildings of the capital in Sacramento testify to the importance of this heartland in the political and social growth of the state.

Richard Dawson

Martin Litton

Josef Muench

William A. Garnett, courtesy
Bank of America N.T. & S.A.

CENTRAL VALLEY (FOLLOWING PAGE)
A green corduroy blanket of crops spreads as far as the eye can see over the immensity of the San Joaquin Valley near Sanger.

CENTRAL VALLEY

The grand scale of agricultural operations creates striking patterns. In a scene of Oriental subtlety, sunlight glances off the shimmering surface of rice ponds contained within gently curving dikes. Elsewhere, in a setting of pure geometry, alternating rows of crops and furrows run to the horizon and vanish there in obedience to the classic laws of perspective.

Verna R. Johnston

CENTRAL VALLEY

Here and there, the grand monotony of horizonless crops, pastures, and orchards is interrupted by park-like vistas that gladden the eye with their natural beauty. The arching valley oaks of Caswell Memorial Park form a shady bower that offers irresistible refuge from the searching sun. In spring a wash of wildflower color sweeps over the great valley from bottom to top, and in Sutter County, acres of golden buttercups spread out beneath oaks just donning their fresh new leaves.

300

CENTRAL VALLEY

Rising in the snow-melt high in the mountains that enclose the great valley, the swift-running rivers carry vessels of all sizes and missions. The towering bulk of a freighter looms among the watchful fishermen like a whale among minnows, as it noses its way down the tule-bordered channel of the Delta, heading for the open sea. At dusk, an outboard cruiser cuts a crisp furrow in the quiet water in front of a darkening river town.

CENTRAL VALLEY

The white sculptured form of the imposing State Capitol (1874), capped by a golden dome, looms above the dark trees and reflects the hot valley sun through the branches. In another part of Sacramento, the Governor's Mansion looks down upon the passing traffic with the starched dignity of an old dowager. Expressive of an earlier day of opulent display, it preserves an air of old-fashioned vigor in the modern, streamlined capital.

The Northern Mountains

Across the top of the state runs a pocket-sized version of the Sierra Nevada, less well known because of its remoteness but deserving of more attention because of its unspoiled grandeur.

This is a land of isolated lakes, where fishermen can cast into wind-ruffled waters that are rarely disturbed by fishhook and leader; of sun-dappled forest trails and wide meadows speckled with wildflowers, inviting alike to hiker and horseman. This is a backpacker's paradise, where faraway campsites can only be reached by foot or on horseback.

Here is the home of the sentinel peaks, Shasta and Lassen, that rise in solitary majesty above the mountain valleys, the southernmost in a long chain of volcanic mountains that stretches to the tip of the Aleutian Islands. Rectangular Mount Shasta, perpetually capped with snow, turns into a solid cake of glistening white in winter and draws skiers flocking to its chair lifts. Mount Lassen, a slumbering volcano that still emits little wisps of steam and sulfurous smoke, rises aloofly above the scenes of the devastation wrought by its eruption in 1915. In the nearby forests that escaped its wrath, its conical form is mirrored in a ring of crystal lakes, some of them bordered by meadows bedecked with blue larkspur and yellow mule ears. In winter, the peak is mantled with heavy snow, which seals off all access until spring.

Perhaps the best known and certainly most accessible of the Northern Mountains' many spectacles is Shasta Lake, an immense, many-fingered body of water that backs up behind a monumental dam. Its irregular shoreline is spotted with campgrounds and boat-launching sites, and its mountainous shores reverberate to a chorus of outboard motors. Waterskiers and sightseers churn the smooth water; and in the quiet coves, fishermen wait expectantly in their motionless boats.

The mountains are densely forested with Douglas fir and pine, much of it marked for logging. The machinegun staccato of chainsaws sounds through the trees, and the narrow forest roads quake with the passing of giant rigs, carrying logs to the distant mills. Rushing rivers flow down the canyons, foaming over the rocks, and fly-fishermen cast into the current, pitting their wiles against the clever trout.

NORTHERN MOUNTAINS (FOLLOWING PAGE)   *Clyde Childress*

Like a bit of Switzerland, the high and rugged Trinity Alps thrust their sharp profiles into the sky. It is late in the season, and the streaked snows are just beginning to recede from the precipitous slopes.

NORTHERN MOUNTAINS

In the snow-free summer, the Trinity's glacial lakes and bosky trails beckon to those willing to leave a car behind. The solitary fisherman casts his line into a lake that is a day's hike from the roadhead. A swamper leads a party along a sun-dappled trail to a drop-camp many jogging miles from care.

310

NORTHERN MOUNTAINS

Mighty Shasta Dam stands with its back braced against the great artificial lake that it created—a pressing 47 square miles of water. Over its concrete spillway and through its penstocks flows the Sacramento River, continuing on its interrupted course. Behind the dam, the many-fingered lake reaches into innumerable wooded inlets, some developed as boat harbors.

312

NORTHERN MOUNTAINS

From the air, the far-ranging water of Shasta Lake catches fire in the dying radiance of the setting sun, in bright contrast to the velvet dark of the mountains. The lake traces an intricate shoreline in all directions and beyond the outermost edge of the visual horizon. In the bright light of day and 50 miles to the north, the mountain that supplies the name for both lake and dam, rears its sugar-loaf bulk above broad wooded valleys, its summit capped with diaphanous clouds.

315

Frances Coleberd

NORTHERN MOUNTAINS

The gray-white, granite domes and spires of Castle Crags rise out of an evergreen forest traversed by the Sacramento River, foaming over a boulder-strewn course. Farther to the east, underground Burney Creek bursts out of the side of a cliff to drop 132 feet to the roiling pool below.

John Robinson

317

Richard Dawson

NORTHERN MOUNTAINS

Awesome evidence of the devastation wrought by eruptions of volcanic Lassen Peak spreads over a moon-like wasteland formed by rockslides that raced down nearby Chaos Crags. In a more innocent mood, snow-covered Lassen, wearing its cold-weather cap of steam, looks down upon tranquil Manzanita Lake.

319

Colophon

This book was printed and bound in San Francisco, California: pages by Stecher-Traung Lithograph Corporation from lithograph film by Balzer-Shopes, cover and jacket by Charles R. Wood & Associates, binding by Cardoza Bookbinding Company. Type composition was done by Kingsport Press of Kingsport, Tennessee, and by Griffin Typographers and Mackenzie & Harris of San Francisco. Paper is Warren's Lustro Offset Enamel.

Cover photographs by Josef Muench.